Key to Awareness

Fiona Maguire

Key to Awareness Manual

© 2011 Fiona Maguire. All rights reserved.

ISBN 978-1-4709-6939-4

Process created by Fiona Maguire

Manual written by Fiona Maguire

Illustrations by Caroline Chapple email:
carolinechapple@aol.com

"Key to Awareness" and this manual is the property of Fiona Maguire, do not copy or distribute without the authors permission.

This book is a print on demand book, to help save paper and trees.

www.RealEnergy4All.com

Contents

Foreword	9
How to use this Manual	13
Introduction	15
Key to Awareness	21
Important Note: Perception	22
Important Note: Motivation	23
Examples, **Example 1**,	30
Example 2, **Example 3**	31
Example 4, **Example 5**	32
How to use the steps in part 1 of the process	33
Step 1	34
'Thinking' people's Key to Awareness	37
Step 2	37
Step 3	40

Self-talk	40
Step 4	43
Step 5	46
Step 6	49
'Feeling' people's Key to Awareness	51
Step 2e	51
Step 3e	54
Step 4e	56
Step 5e	60
Step 6e	64
Being Triggered	66
Acceptance	67
Noticing thought(s) and emotion(s) together	71
Step 7	71
Step 8	75

Step 9 81

Part 2 83

Appendixes 141

References 147

Foreword

I created this easy to follow process to help people stop the chaos and suffering in their lives that I went through by not being aware. Awareness of yourself and what is happening around you gives you the freedom to be who you are and express yourself in everything you do. If you want to be **free, happy** and **energised everyday follow this process to awareness.**

"Key to Awareness" is a simple practical process that guides you in how to become more aware as you go about your normal everyday activities. Part 1 of "Key to Awareness" guides you **step by step** to becoming more aware of your thoughts, emotions and actions. Then you are guided in how you can enable your thoughts, emotions and actions to be more in align with your true self and be directed from your intuition. This is how you create the Life You want to Life.

Part 2 of "Key to Awareness" guides you through 'exercises' that enable you to release tension and conditioning i.e. what is blocking you in your body and mind that has been created through unhelpful moods, conditioning and trauma.

In this process, and therefore manual, I am not asking you to take on any of my or anyone else's beliefs. All I ask of you is

to go through the process **step by step** and write down on the tables provided what you notice and **practise the exercises** given in part 2 of the manual. This manual is **a practical process that leads you to becoming aware**; rather than a manual that contains just the philosophy of awareness.

This process is to assist you in becoming aware and present in your own being.

Being aware **creates a space inside yourself**, which is created by noticing your thoughts and emotions and **releasing the tension and conditioning inside your body**. Awareness enables you to be present in the moment; being present in the moment enables a deeper awareness. In awareness you become present to your inner guidance and you will intuitively know what to do and how to do it; there is no need for thoughts / decision-making as your actions flow from within you and out into the world. Awareness is a process that develops in you as you listen and act upon your intuitive knowing.

When awareness is brought to unhelpful emotions and thoughts and you return to the present moment, where there is no room for unhelpful emotions and thoughts, they just naturally fade away. The **benefit of becoming and acting from your true self is <u>much less</u>,** if any, **procrastination, frustration, indecision, worry, fear** and other unhelpful emotions and thoughts.

What is Awareness?

Awareness is fundamentally noticing your thoughts, feelings, emotions and actions; what is happening inside you, and what is happening around you. Then **allow yourself to accept them.** Awareness is needed to get to know yourself. Acceptance is needed to enable yourself to develop and change the parts of yourself and your life that you would like to. **Awareness and acceptance work best together.**

This means that you allow yourself to feel and think whatever it is that you are feeling and thinking in any moment; no matter if these emotions and thoughts are around being angry and fearful or happy and extremely joyful.

Therefore if you feel angry notice that you are angry and accept it. If you have already started to express the anger also bring your awareness to how you are expressing that anger. Jumping up and down and shouting, if you are by yourself, may be at this moment the best way you have of expressing your anger and the quickest way you have of releasing it. However, if you are with other people learning a different way to express and release your anger may be a better option. Being aware of yourself and what is happening around you gives you more options in how you express yourself and more options in life in general.

As you go through this process of noticing your thoughts, emotions and actions, you will come to realise that they are there to serve who you believe yourself to be. These beliefs have come from your 'conditioning'. Conditioning is what you have been taught to do by your parents, family, friends, groups you interact with, the media and society in general.

You can only change and break free from your conditioning by becoming aware of what your conditioning is.

Awareness is not a passive way of being; it is more than just noticing that you are doing something. Once you have noticed that you are doing something become aware of your motivation for doing it. You do this by noticing what thoughts and emotions you have before, during and after the action. If you choose to keep doing the activity and having the same thoughts and emotions about it, **remember this is your choice**.

I have heard people say that I cannot help it, it is just the way I am; at least I am aware of it. This is just a poor excuse and they are not aware, they have just simply noticed that they often repeat the same behaviour. If this reminds you of yourself or someone you know the good news is that **repeated behaviour that is not positive** for you and / or the people around you is **probably motivated by conditioning**.

With true awareness you will realize that you are not the conditioning and you will begin to let go of it. When you are present in awareness your true self will emerge, which is free from conditioning and you will feel free, liberated and empowered and act from your true self intuitively. **This is the purpose of "Key to Awareness".**

How to use this manual

This manual needs to be read in the order that it is set out in. Some sections of the manual refer to other sections and this is indicated in the text.

Part 1 of this process is divided into nine steps that progress from one to the other. **It is important that you follow each step in order.** There are guidelines about how you progress through the steps in the 'How to use the steps in part 1 of the process' section. **To get the most out of this process please follow these guidelines.**

You can start practising the exercises in part 2 of the manual once you have started the steps in part 1 of the manual.

There are *__Important Notes:__* throughout the text, which are there to bring your attention to an important point that has either been made or needs to be brought to your attention at that moment. Spend time considering the 'Important Notes'. You may find it helpful to reread the 'Important Notes' in each section before you move onto the next section.

__Important Note:__

*If the same pattern of thoughts or emotions are arising from one step to another and you are repeating the same or very similar actions; please note that **you may be stuck on a previous step**. If this happens, return to the step where you first notice the thought or emotional pattern. Reread the step and look at what you have written on the table that corresponds with the step. See if any insights arise from doing this?*

It may help to stay with this step and notice what you are asked to for the next few days as you go about your normal everyday activities. If the pattern is related to something in particular, for example your work or a relationship, it is important that you experience this as part of this step. This may mean that you stay with the step for longer than a few days, to enable you to see the person or go to work, for example. **See 'An example of how someone became aware of how they were stuck' in the appendixes.**

Introduction

Studying psychology, religions, different spiritual paths, and many body and mind based therapies, seeing hundreds of clients over the years and my own personal experience has brought me to one conclusion: **Awareness is all that is needed to create the life You want.**

Before You can create the life that you want you need to know

What You are doing?

and what You want to do?

People often experience answering these questions as difficult because they are unaware of how their unconscious mind is affecting them. Our unconscious mind contains all the programming and conditioning that we have collected from our parents, family, loved ones, advertising, the media and society. **Basically there is nothing in the world that does not feed us with information that we store in our unconscious mind and are then directly or indirectly influence by it.**

There are a few people in the world that are "blissfully" unaware that they can have an impact on their own life and they put up with whatever "life throws at them". This is not to say that these people are necessary happy, or unhappy, they **probably do not even realise that they have options.**

You are probably not one of these people. You probably sense that there is more to life than what you are presently experiencing; otherwise you would not be reading this manual. Sometimes you may feel that this is not true and doubt your ability to create a more fulfilling life for yourself. **These self doubts and self sabotaging thoughts** are likely to be the **result of how you are viewing the world at the moment.**

Are you:

1. Stuck in your head replaying events from the past over and over again like a broken record?
2. Stuck in fear or worrying about what will happen in the future?
3. So busy planning for the future, you are not paying attention to what is happening right now?

This is ironic because <u>what you do</u>

or <u>do not do now,</u>

<u>determines the future.</u>

The trap of today's modern way of life is that we become stuck on the treadmill; that is we are constantly in **'doing mode'**. You are programmed to believe that happiness, contentment, peace of mind and ... (insert whatever you yearn for) is found outside of yourself, in something you buy, a level of status or at some future point. **There is no future point where you are going to suddenly think and feel this is it I've arrive, I'm happy, I have everything I want.**

What you are yearning for and the truth of who you are is only to be found in awareness in this moment and every moment. Awareness of what you are thinking and feeling and what is happening around you. You can connect with all of this **with awareness and acceptance and with a light heartedness; in this you will be happy, free and have peace of mind.**

Key to Awareness will give you the tools in an easy to follow <u>step by step</u> way to open up this in you. I congratulate you for choosing to go on this journey of self discovery. **Let me know what happens at <u>www.RealEnergy4All.com</u>**

Below is the **'story'** of how I created this process:

In January 2005 I fell over on ice and fractured my right radius near my wrist. Apart from this being very painful at times it was also very restrictive to what I was physically capable of doing. As I could not drive a car or write I could not go to the contract I was working on at the time and I could definitely not massage people. Cooking with one hand was a challenge that I managed by being creative with what I bought to cook.

As a result I had a lot of time to meditate and reflect on my life. What I realised was that even though I was earning more money than I had ever done before, was living in my own mortgaged house, was seeing someone and had good friends, I was not happy. **My life was so busy before that that I had not realised, even in meditation, that I was not happy.** I had always had the thought and feeling that there is more to life than what I saw my parents and other people doing with their lives. However, here I was at 30 years old with everything that my parents and society said I should have and it did not make me happy.

My belief at the time, that I believe was influenced mainly from Buddhism, was that freedom is obtained through non-self, which I took to mean 'having no identity'. What happened was that I sold my house and moved into a Buddhist temple to deepen my Buddhist practice and see what would happen.

In the temple I realised how judgemental I was and how my sarcastic sense of humour was judgemental and hurtful to others. I decided to leave the temple after being there for two months. I left with an altered sense of humour and a stronger belief that the true me would reveal itself if I was to strip away all the labels that made up my identity. **Please note that this was my misunderstanding of Buddhist teachings.**

In all I spent just under three years searching for a deep understanding of who I was and another way of living in which I would become free to express who I am. I learnt many things about myself and learnt some new ways of reading and working with energy. Over time I managed to **lose my labels along with my sense of identity. The result of this was that I became depressed and cried a lot.** I quickly realised that I needed the support of my family and friends and decided to move back to my home town. I started massaging people again and realised that I had missed it and that I am happy when I am helping people feel better.

Overall I learnt that I love to meditate and just be and I also love to be active helping people and myself. In other words I learnt balance. Most importantly I learnt:

I become free when I allow myself to be aware of my thoughts and emotions and by accepting myself, I can express who I am in whatever I do; this is freedom and it is liberating and empowering.

In reflecting on everything I have studied and on my own life experiences as a fellow being and therapist, I have created this process.

This process enables You to have greater and more choices in your life, rather then acting out of a sense of what is expected from you by your family, peers and society. When we do this we often put what is important to us aside and can act unconsciously out of habit (which may leave you thinking and feeling like you have no choice in your life).

By practising Key to Awareness you will become aware.

Being aware creates a space inside yourself, which is created by noticing your thoughts and emotions and releasing the tension and conditioning inside your body. Then **who you really are can arise and you will intuitively know what to do and how to do it.**

You are the awareness.

Awareness, which includes acceptance, is all that is needed to be balanced, free and happy.

What follows is an explanation of the process. After this, there is a detailed guide of each of the steps that make up part 1 of the process.

Key to Awareness

Key to Awareness is divided into two parts. **The first part is becoming more aware** of your thought(s), emotion(s), thought patterns and emotional patterns and how these affect your actions. It is divided into nine steps that progress from one to the other.

The second part is about processing the energy in your body that is caused by your thought(s) and emotion(s) and conditioning and thus **releasing it.**

You are not your thoughts. You are not your emotions. You are not your actions. The common misconception that you are your thoughts, emotions and actions is what can cause the conflict inside of you and often results in the uneasiness you feel.

You are the awareness.

I encourage you to work through the process **step by step** using the table that corresponds with the step to record what happens in each step. This will help you become aware of your conditioning and thought and emotional patterns quickly and easily.

You need to be aware of something either consciously which is what part 1 will assist you in becoming, or physically which is what part 2 will assist you in becoming, in order to be able to change and or release it. **For very old conditioning and stubborn patterns**, in my experience with myself and clients, **a conscious acknowledgement and a physical release of the** old conditioning and stubborn patterns are needed to release and / or change them.

Becoming aware will change the way you perceive and experience yourself (your internal world) and the external world, so that you will have more clarity and energy and be able to see and make changes easily when you may need to.

Important Note: Perception

Perception is the mental process of how we make sense of the world and our experiences in the world. Our perception is often the result of our internal world i.e. what we think, feel, our memories of our past experiences and the knowledge we have, rather than what is reality. To get an idea that perception is more about your internal world ask a friend about something that happened yesterday that you experienced together. It will not be unusual that your friend's perception and therefore memory of the situation will be very different from yours.

Your perception will determine what you pay attention to internally and externally in any given situation. This means that your perception is filtered by your thoughts, emotions, past experiences, knowledge and values. It is important to notice that we also filter what we allow ourselves to consciously think and feel; we hide our painful and scary thoughts and emotions from even ourselves. What we allow ourselves to notice we often unconsciously decide so quickly and act as quickly that we never give ourselves chance to see if there is another option. Have you ever had the experience where you have felt excited and happy to do something and you may have even briefly noticed that there is something about the possibility of doing it that does not feel right (people often say that this is their gut feeling) or that it may not be all it seems to be. Suddenly you find yourself doing it and then it goes wrong, and you ask yourself why!

With awareness you pay attention to all of you and by accepting all of it and allowing it time to settle your true self knows what to do. In my experience what I have then done 9 out of 10 times was exactly the right thing for me to do. On the occasions where something has gone wrong I am able, with awareness, to learn a valuable lesson and bring this lesson forward into my life and recover, if I need to, very quickly.

To summarise the Key to Awareness process will help you become aware of your filters to perceiving what is really happening. Awareness is perceiving what is actually happening inside of you and around you, rather than seeing the world through your filters of habitual thought, emotional and behavioural patterns. These habitual patterns are often the result of your conditioning. Conditioning is what you have been taught to do by your parents, family, friends, groups you interact with, the media and society in general. **You can only change and break free from 'your' conditioning by becoming aware of what 'your' conditioning is.**

Being able to consciously experience our thoughts and emotions is a fundamental part of being human. People often have the **misconception that aware people either do not feel or think 'unhelpful' or 'bad'** things or if they do they definitely do not allow themselves to express them. **I have fallen into this trap myself** and have experienced it with many other people. This just leads to built up tension and uneasiness and in my personal experience led to depression. **Awareness is being aware of and accepting your thoughts and emotions and enabling your true self to express itself.**

Your actions are often perceived by others as demonstrating who you are; they are at best just a representation of who you are. The interaction between your thoughts, emotions and actions can often effect your perception of yourself and the interactions you have with the outside world. **This interaction with the outside world is no different from the interaction you have with yourself i.e. it can be easy or it can be chaotic and cause conflict. The choice is yours and only yours.**

Important Note: Motivation

All of your actions are a result of what is motivating you. *Would you do anything if you did not have a goal in mind as to why you were doing it? Your actions can be motivated by values, beliefs or a desire to get something for yourself or someone else. I believe that when we are completely honest with ourselves we notice that all our actions our motivated by a desire to help ourselves, even if we 'believe' we are doing something to help someone else. Think about the last time you did something for someone else? Can you honestly say that there was not any reason for doing it that did not help you in some way? Your motivation might have come out of the desire to avoid criticism or judgement, or maybe you wanted to be seen as 'a good person'.*

I would like you to keep in mind what is motivating your actions as you work through this process. In step 6 you are asked to look at your tables and your experiences and reflect on what motivates you.

No one else can control your thoughts, emotions and actions. An important part of Key to Awareness is that you also let go of controlling your thoughts and emotions. This means that you do not suppress or deny them. Instead you **allow** whatever **thoughts and emotions arise and you accept them.** What I mean by acceptance is allowing your thoughts and emotions to be how they are **without adding extra** to them, by fighting, judging, blaming, analysing, making a story etc, (more about <u>Acceptance</u> below). Awareness is allowing and accepting your thoughts and emotions and often this is all that is needed to release them.

By becoming aware you become more at ease and happier in yourself. This is the purpose of Key to Awareness and with practice you will achieve this more aware way of being.

Important Note:

Awareness is needed to get to know yourself. Acceptance is needed to enable yourself to develop and change the parts of you and your life that you would like to. Awareness and acceptance work best together.

Awareness is allowing and accepting your thoughts and emotions; often this is all that is needed to release them.

Throughout the day you have thoughts and feelings all the time. Some people may be aware of their thoughts more than what they feel and for other people they are more aware of their feelings. I believe that thoughts and feelings arise in the body together and the majority of thoughts have feelings that accompany them and the majority of feelings have thoughts that accompany them. When feelings become strong enough they become emotions (Edward de Bono; Vermilion., 2004).

People can get confused by what is an emotion and what is a thought. For example in a session I had with a lady, lets call her Clair, she said "The emotions are Sadness and it's unfair". Sadness is an emotion, but 'it's unfair' is a thought. **This demonstrates that thoughts and emotions are experienced together and do accompany each other, because they so strongly affect each other.** However, often people do believe that they are either more aware of their thoughts and are therefore 'thinking' people or they believe they are more aware of their emotions and believe themselves to be 'feeling' people.

Important Note:

In the society that we live in today what you think and logical reasoning is most likely to be perceived as being superior to everything else. Pressure is placed on everyone to think and be seen as being intelligent. This is demonstrated in all the "I think..." statements people use and the phrases people use: "What were you thinking?"... "Where was your mind? These questions can be difficult for anyone to answer and more so for a person who is more keenly aware of their emotions. However, the chances are that everyone's mind is working and coming up with thoughts all day long, whether we are aware of them or not. Just close your eyes for a minute and listen to how many thoughts arise.

Thought and emotion, if you are unaware, tend to go in cycles. That is, a thought will often lead to another thought and an emotion will often lead to another emotion. It is useful to become aware that your thought and emotions do cycle and which ones lead to action, as a means of being able to stop unhelpful cycles before they led to actions. However, it is **not important** once you become aware that you are in a cycle to know what thoughts or emotions lead too or came before the point of which you became aware of the cycle.

It is **not important** to get to what some people call the underlying or bottom emotion / thought. I believe that this technique often causes people to become stuck in a cycle of negative emotions /thoughts. Alternatively it can lead people into endless analysing of their thoughts, 'stories' and themselves.

Important Note:

The Key to Awareness process is about releasing thoughts, emotions, conditioning and habits that do not serve you. So that you become aware, have clarity and are guided by your inner wisdom.

A thought or emotion might be linked to a certain situation and then cycle off to a totally unrelated situation; when this happens you will often forget what you were thinking about, or feeling, in the first place. Alternatively they can cycle as a result of a particular situation, as in **example 1**. This can continue for a while and will result in an unconscious action, see **example 2**. Your action may be out of habit if you are not aware of either your thoughts or emotions. Your habitual thoughts and emotions lead to the same habitual actions.

Important Note:

If you always do what you have always done, you will always get the same result. This most likely means that you will continue to experience the same chaos and suffering in your life over and over again.

All you need to do to stop the cycle is to become aware of a thought or an emotion. The instant you become aware you create a gap in the cycle that will often stop the cycle completely. Whilst you are developing awareness and acceptance it is helpful, when this gap has been created, to choose another thought or feeling that is more likely to lead to a more beneficial action, see **example 3**.

Through using the nine steps of part one of the Key to Awareness process you are guided **step by step** into becoming more aware of your thoughts and emotions. The first four steps of this process are to get you to notice your habitual responses and conditioning; as you need to be aware of how you react to let go of the need to react. The rest of the process gives you tools to respond rather than react. Whilst you are developing this awareness you will then use the techniques in part 2 of the process to go inside yourself and release unhelpful thought and emotions. Your action will then be more aligned with who you are and what you want to create in your life, see **example 4.**

By step 8 you will be more present in who you really are and will have a deep sense of knowing what is needed in that moment, **see example 5**.

Important Note:

As you go through the process step by step your awareness grows and you will start to notice that you will go inside yourself more to find out what your truth is in that moment and connect with your deep sense of knowing.

Awareness is a process that keeps developing in you.

Examples

The situation for the following example is a project that you have been working on has come to a stop and it does not seem to be going anywhere, i.e. you do not have any new sales, your clients have stopped coming, no one is interested. What follows is a typical self dialogue you might experience in this situation and maybe on a more regular basis. It is an example of how a thought leads to another thought and an emotion leads to another emotion. Furthermore, it is an example of how thought and emotion accompany each other.

Example 1

Thoughts	Accompanying	Emotions
I get so far	/	Disappointment
then it all falls apart		Anger
↓		↓
Life is a struggle	/	Hopelessness
↓		↓
What's the point!	/	Despair

In the society we live in today we are often expected to act instantly under pressure. As explained, our action will be strongly influenced by our thoughts and our emotions. If you are unaware of your thoughts or emotions you may act out of habit and therefore repeat what you have always done, as in the example below:

Example 2

Thought = 'What's the point!' accompanying Emotion = Despair, Habitual Action = Give up – let everything that you have done go.

This habitual reaction is common in people that have the conditioning 'Life is a struggle'. The result of this habitual thought is often that they start to believe that everything is hard work and they will never achieve satisfaction and joy from anything they do.

Example 3

Thought = 'What's the point!', unaware accompanying Emotion = Despair. Awareness of thought creates a gap in which you can choose another thought = 'Lets look at what I have achieved', Action = Review what you have achieved and done to see what you can do to bring the project forward.

With the awareness you have at this moment, this new chosen thought is more likely to lead to a more beneficial action. If you are unaware of the emotion or are trying to deny it, the emotion will probably negatively affect your motivation and the believe you have in doing the action well and to the best of your ability.

Example 4

Thought = 'What's the point!', aware accompanying Emotion = Despair. **You then go inside of yourself, part 2 of the process, and release the emotion of despair and connect with the emotion that you had at the start of the project, for example enthusiasm.**

By doing this you are more likely to find the solution that will bring the project forward again or you may happily realise that you need to do something else, using the skills that you have learnt by doing the project.

Example 5

Thought = 'What's the point!', aware accompanying Emotion = Despair. **You then go inside of yourself, part 2 of the process, and be present in your deep sense of knowing.** Action = What is needed in that moment for you to express who you really are in that moment:

This is how you Create the Life You want to Live!

How to use the steps in part 1 of the process:

Part 1 of this process is divided into nine steps that progress from one to the other. <u>It is important that you follow each step in order.</u> I would recommend that you:

- Read the steps in the order that they are given and do not read any other steps until you have completed the previous step. If you know what is coming in the next step this will probably influence what you notice.

- Spend a few days on each step.

- Read the step through, taking in what it is asking you to notice; try to avoid evaluating the step. Any questions that you may have will probably be answered by carry out the step.

- Go about your day noticing what is laid out in each step.

- Record what you notice on the table that is provided with each step.

- If you are already following a daily practice to help you become more aware, please continue it.

- However, if you have just started a practice, I would recommend only following this manual. This is to help you be clear with what you are noticing and the benefits of the process.

You can start practising the exercises in part 2 of the manual once you have started the steps in part 1 of the manual.

Step 1

To make it easier to notice your habits and conditioning I encourage you to work with whatever you are more comfortable with at first. Therefore if you believe that you are a 'thinking' person work with your thoughts or if you believe you are more of a 'feeling' person work with your emotions.

Important Note:

If you are unsure of the answer to this question, it really does not matter. The only purpose of this is to make it easier for you to notice one thing, your thoughts or your emotions at first. By step 5 or 6 you will automatically start to notice the other anyway and are encouraged to in step 7.

Are you a thinking person? When describing yourself do you say "I think ..."? Do you spend your time in your head always thinking and analysing what is happening, or happened or about to happen?

A thought is the words and or images you hear and see in your head. If you believe this is you go to the

'Thinking' people's Key to Awareness.

Alternatively, are you a 'feeling' person who acts from their emotions and follows their gut feeling when taking action. When describing yourself do you say "I feel..."?

When feelings become strong enough they become emotions. Emotions are usually felt and located in the body and for this reason 'feeling' people are usually more in touch with their bodies than 'thinking' people. Each emotion can often be described by a single word i.e. sad, happy, angry, lonely, safe etc. We are capable of feeling more than one emotion at a time. If you believe this is you go to the

'Feeling' people's Key to Awareness.

Important Note:

What leads your actions and decisions?

I would recommend contemplating this step for a day and notice what does actually lead your actions and decisions?

For example, I am a person who does think deeply about things and I do like to plan. However, it is my emotions that I listen to more and they lead my actions and decisions. Therefore, I consider myself to be more a 'feeling' person.

Start the process after one day of contemplating this question; it does not matter what you start with, as long as you start.

Please go to the Key to Awareness section for you:

'Thinking people's' Key to Awareness

Step 2

If you are more aware of your thoughts, you start by noticing your thoughts, especially the thoughts that you have regularly. At first it may be helpful to write down your thoughts (use table 1 below). As previously mentioned people have thoughts going through their minds almost constantly.

The thoughts that I am asking you to become aware of are the thoughts that are adding to the essence of what you are doing, or are sabotaging what you are doing. The sabotaging thoughts seem to pop out of nowhere and can lead us to not completing the task to the best of our ability or to a different unhelpful action.

For example a person at work is finding it difficult to complete a task; the thought is 'I cannot ask my boss for help, he will think I'm stupid.' This thought is likely to lead the person into making mistakes and taking much longer than necessarily to complete the task. Furthermore, as they may have not learnt anything from the experience they are likely to have reinforced their thought and maybe they will start to believe they are stupid.

Important Note:

*As previously mentioned, noticing something without bringing extra to it is often all that is required to release it (see **Acceptance** below for more information).*

Table 1: Notice regular thoughts.

Date and time	Situation	Thought(s)	What did you notice?
Example	Finding it difficult to complete a task.	I cannot ask my boss for help, he will think I'm stupid.	I made mistakes, it took me longer to complete the task. I feel more stupid now.

Step 3

Next try to notice what thoughts tend to lead to other thoughts, which are your thought patterns (see **example 1** above), and what actions they lead too. Write these down using 2, below.

Important Note:

As part of this step pay attention to the words you use when talking to others. What we say often reveals the beliefs that we have and therefore our internal and external perceptions.

Also pay attention to your **self-talk**, i.e. how you talk to yourself. I have not met anyone who does not talk to themselves. If I want to say something to someone that I feel is important or sensitive I will often have the conversation in my head first to see if it 'sounds' the way that I would like it to. Self-talk is also a great way to remember things. However, when I started to pay attention to my self-talk I could not believe how often it was telling me off, calling me names and criticising me. Sometimes I would 'hear' my self-talk in my own voice and sometimes it would be in someone else's, which was often one of my parents' voices. I believe my self-talk was the reason why I would sometimes feel in a 'bad' or 'negative' mood and not know why.

Listening to my self-talk made me realise many unconscious beliefs I had about myself, other people and the world. At first I thought that some were rather trivial, like I would hear "clumsy" when I dropped something or made a minor mistake. My first response was to laugh. However, to my surprise when I paid attention to how I felt I realised that I felt criticised and told off. This is not trivial at all, because if I did not allow time to notice and accept these feelings fully and allow them to be released, my body would hold onto these feelings and they would be more easily triggered in the near future, more about being triggered in **step 4** and **Being Triggered** below.

Important Note:

I have seen with my clients that it is often their self-talk that leads to negativity and mood swings that further causes them chaos and suffering.

I guess for more 'thinking' people they might start analysing if they are clumsy or not, in the back of their mind. When I have done this I have found it extremely tiring and it takes me away from being in awareness. For example, a belief that many of my clients had when they first came to see me, is that 'I am unworthy'. Any time the client would have this thought they would instantly go into analysing their life story to see what experiences they have had that support this thought 'I am unworthy' and try to convince me that it is true. A quick counter technique to this sabotaging thought is to remind yourself of experiences that do not support the thought. This may help to create some space and in this space awareness may arise. However, analysing without any room for space usually delays, if not prevents, pure awareness.

Table 2 - Thought cycles and patterns.

Date and time	Situation	Thought that lead to next thought	What did you notice?
Example	The project I have been working on has come to a stop.	I get so far and then it all falls apart	The thoughts followed each other so quickly.
		Life's a struggle	
		What's the point!	

Step 4

If you find yourself doing something without any previous awareness of thoughts, let yourself notice what you are thinking at that moment. Then see if you can remember what thought led you to the action you are doing now and took you away from the action you were doing. For example you were doing a task that you are familiar with and you find yourself fantasising about being somewhere else (could be on holiday, in a different job, living somewhere else etc) your conscious thought at that moment is 'This is great'. You then remember that the thoughts that took you away from your task were 'I'm bored. I no longer enjoy doing this'. Record this on table 3 below.

Important Note:

You are trying to remember the one recent thought that took you away from the task that you were doing. The purpose of this is to find out what habitual thought(s) are less than positive for you.

Alternatively you may have been triggered. Being triggered is when you start to act, think and feel as if the original experience, which could have happened a long time ago and caused a major reaction in you at the time of that experience, is happening again in this moment. The original experience was also probably traumatising.

The example that is given in **table 3** is that you find yourself shouting "What do you mean!" to a colleague at work. Your conscious thought at that moment is 'How dare he laugh at me'. You remember that the thought that took you away from previously having a laugh and a joke with your colleagues was that "He is bullying me". On reflection you realise that you were triggered, by your colleague laughing at you, back to thinking and behaving as if you were back at school and being bullied.

It is especially useful to keep a record of the situations where you have become triggered (**use table 3**). At the end of this section please read the section on **"Being Triggered"**.

With the practice of bringing awareness into your life you will notice when you have become triggered and will come out of it more quickly and return to balance. When you are familiar with both parts of Key to Awareness you will be much less likely to be triggered.

The aim is to become aware of the chaos and suffering that is created by your habitual reactions. Through practicing this process you develop more options and balance in your life.

Table 3: Notice what thoughts took you away from what you were doing.

Date and time	Situation What are you doing now?	Present Thought(s)	What were you Doing?	What thoughts took you away from what you were doing?
Example	Shouting "What do you mean!" to a colleague	How dare he laugh at me	Having a laugh and a joke with your colleagues at work.	He is bullying me 'triggered' me back to school were I was bullied.

Step 5

Is it becoming easier to notice your thoughts? Have you noticed that when you become aware of your thoughts, your thoughts momentarily stop? It is the awareness of the thought(s) that creates the gap in your thinking. In this gap you can choose another thought that is likely to lead to a more aware and thus beneficial action. Choosing another thought opens up your old patterns of thinking and starts to break down your conditioning. **See examples 1 to 3**. Record when you do this on table 4, below.

Important Note:

Choosing another thought is a useful tool whilst you are developing awareness and acceptance. The ability to choose another thought comes out of being aware and is a step towards Pure Awareness; however, it is not Pure Awareness. In Pure Awareness your actions flow through you, from the space of you being present in your own being.

Another example is that you are dissatisfied in your job. Your thoughts might go something like this

I don't want to go >>> How else can I >>>I don't know what I
to work   pay my bills   want / can do

Normal action = Go to work and complain about work to yourself and others.

Awareness of thought = I don't know what I want / can do?' creates a gap and you choose to another thought = 'What do I like doing?', leads to action = Notice what you like doing at work and what gives you joy and satisfaction in work and away from work.

Table 4: Choosing another thought to lead to a more beneficial action.

Date and time	Situation	Thought that lead to next Thought	What Thought did you choose?	Action.
Example	I'm dissatisfied in my job.	I don't want to go to work		
		How else can I pay my bills?		Notice what you like doing and what gives you joy and satisfaction in work and outside of work.
		I don't know what I want / can do	What do I like doing?	

Step 6

Reflect on your thought(s) and actions to see whether you could have chosen another thought that would have been more helpful, that would lead to an action that would be more in alignment with who you are - your true self. Reflect on what you have written on **Tables 1 to 4**.

It is helpful to step back and reflect on what your motivation for being in the situation was and what your motivation for choosing the thought in step 5 was. You may believe that you had to choose the thought so fast that you did not have time to consider what your motivation was. However as I have stated in the **'Important Note: Motivation'** all of your actions are a result of what is motivating you. To become aware of what was motivating you notice what thoughts you had before, during and after the action.

Try to avoid justifying and analysing your thoughts and actions and what is motivating them. Try to settle inside of yourself and ask yourself "What was I trying to achieve? What in me was guiding my thoughts and actions?" Allow the answer to arise from within you. Take your time and be honest with yourself. Acceptance of all that is arising within you is needed here. To help you do this look at part 2 of the manual, especially the part on Grounding. When you are grounded a space is created inside of you that enables you to be present and connected to your inner guidance and knowing.

Using the example above in **step 5** when you have noticed what you like doing, you also need to take action if you want to change your experience of your job or if you choose to find a new job that you will feel motivated to do. Therefore, in the gap you choose another thought 'What are my options?' which leads to action = consider options and find out more information. You may be able to do this by yourself using the support network that you have around you and you could also speak to, for example, a professional life coach or careers advisor.

Over the next couple of days practice going inside of yourself and asking yourself "What was I trying to achieve? What in me was guiding my thoughts and actions?" Allow the answer to arise from within you. Take your time and be honest with yourself.

Important Note:

Please read the ***"Being Triggered"*** and ***"Acceptance"*** sections below. After reading theses sections please continue to step 7 and follow each step to the end of the process. Steps 7 through to 9 are the same for 'thinking people' and 'feeling people' as they bring awareness of emotions and thoughts together.

'Feeling' people's Key to Awareness

Step 2e

If you are more aware of your emotions and feelings you start by noticing your emotions. You may be aware that it is not unusual to experience more than one emotion at a time and this is perfectly normal.

Notice and write down what emotions you tend to experience together and what action they lead to (use table 1e, below). Pay attention to sabotaging emotions, which seem to pop out of nowhere and can lead us to not completing the task to the best of our ability or lead to a completely different unhelpful action. For example a person at work is finding it difficult to complete a task; the emotions are inferiority and not 'being' good enough. These emotions are likely to lead the person into making mistakes and taking much longer than necessary to complete the task. Furthermore, as they may not have learnt anything from the experience they are likely to have reinforced their self sabotaging emotions.

Important Note: 'feeling person'

If you are more of a 'feeling person' you may experience your feelings and emotions very deeply. This can make it difficult to determine if what you are feeling is your emotion or someone else's emotion. It is not unusual for 'feeling people' to pick up on and feel other people's emotions; this can be a very useful skill in knowing how to relate to people. However if we take on someone else's emotion and believe that it is ours, we can suddenly experience ourselves feeling bad, angry, upset etc. when previously we were happy and having a great day.

It is always useful to 'go inside of yourself' and ask if what you are feeling is yours or someone else's emotion(s). Trust the answer you get; as you progress through this process your trust will grow and you will become more aware of when you have taken on someone else's emotion(s). One of the benefits of this process is that you will be much less likely to take on others' emotion(s).

Table 1e: Regular emotions.

Date and time	Situation	Emotion(s)	What did you notice?
Example	Finding it difficult to complete a task.	Inferiority and not good enough.	I made mistakes, it took me longer to complete the task. I feel more inferior now

Step 3e

Next try to notice what emotions tend to lead to other emotions and write them down (use table 2e below). For example if you have the emotion(s) of disappointment and anger these might lead to feelings of hopelessness, which might lead to feelings of despair; this is an emotional pattern (see **example 1**). Write down on table 2e what action your emotional patterns lead to. The example that I have given above in **example 1** and in **table 2e** is that this emotional pattern leads to you giving up – letting everything that you have done go.

Important Note:

*Please read the Important Notes about talking to others and **self talk** under **step 3** of 'Thinking people's' Key to Awareness.*

Table 2e: Emotional cycles and patterns.

Date and time	Situation	Emotion(s) that lead to next Emotion(s)	What did you notice?
Example	The project I have been working on has come to a stop.	Dissapointment and Anger	
		Hoplessness	
		Dispair	Give up – let everything that I have done go.

Step 4e

If you find yourself doing something without any previous awareness of emotions, let yourself notice what emotion(s) and feelings you are experiencing at that moment. Then see if you can remember what emotion(s) led you to the action you are doing now and took you away from the action you were doing. For example you were doing a task that you are familiar with and you find yourself fantasising about being somewhere else (could be on holiday, in a different job, living somewhere else etc) your conscious emotions at that moment are joy and happiness. You then remember that the emotions that took you away from your task were dissatisfaction and demotivated. Record this on **table 3e**, below.

Alternatively you may have been triggered. Being triggered is when you start to act, feel and think as if the original experience, that could of happened a long time ago and caused a major reaction in you at the time of that experience, is happening again in this moment. The original experience was also probably traumatising.

The example that is given in **table 3e** is that you find yourself shouting at a colleague at work in front of other colleagues. Your present emotions are angry and upset. You then remember what happened and the emotion that took you away from previously having a laugh and a joke with your colleagues was one of anger. On reflection you realise that you were triggered, by your colleague laughing at you, back to feeling and behaving as if you were back at school and being bullied.

awareness = balance

It is especially useful to keep a record of the situations where you have become triggered (use table 3e). At the end of this section please read the section on **"Being Triggered"**.

Important Note:

As emotions are felt in the body and 'feeling' people often experience their emotions deeply it can be easier for strong emotions, rather than thoughts, to be triggered.

Furthermore, the location in the body of different emotions can be very close together i.e. excitement is often felt in the heart area and fear can often be felt in the solar plexus and / or heart area. Therefore when triggered you can go from one emotion i.e. excitement, to its opposing emotion very quickly i.e. fear.

With the practice of bringing awareness into your life you will notice when you have become triggered and will come out of it quicker. When you are familiar with both parts of Key to Awareness you will be much less likely to be triggered.

The aim is to become aware of the chaos and suffering that is created by your habitual reactions. Through practicing this process you develop more options and balance in your life.

Table 3e: Notice what Emotion(s) took you away from what you were doing.

Date and time	Situation What are you doing now?	Present Emotion(s)	What were you Doing?	What emotion(s) took you away from what you were doing?
Example	Shouting "What do you mean!" to a colleague	Angery and upset	Having a laugh and a joke with your colleagues at work.	Anger I was triggered back to school days.

Step 5e

Is it becoming easier to notice your emotions and the effect of your emotions? Have you noticed that when you become aware of your emotion(s) that it feels like your emotion(s) momentarily stop? It is the awareness of the emotion(s) that creates the gap in them. In this gap you can choose another emotion that is likely to lead to a more aware and thus beneficial action. See **examples 1 to 3** above. Record when you have done this on **table 4e**, below.

Another example is you are dissatisfied in your job. Your emotions might go something like this:

Dissatisfaction >> Security (from pay) >> Fear and apathetic

and 'stuckness'

Normal action = Go to work and feel worse.

Awareness of emotion = Fear and apathetic, creates a gap and you choose another emotion = Curiosity, which leads to action = Notice what you like doing at work and what gives you joy and satisfaction in work and away from work.

If you think it is impossible to decide to feel another emotion try this exercise. Remember a recent episode in your life in which you felt a little sad. After a short period of time, stand up, look up and smile. What are you feeling now? The majority of people feel happy after they have stood up and smiled whilst looking up.

Another exercise that you can try is that you can practise feeling emotions that feel good. You do this by remembering a time when you were really happy, or another emotion that you would like to be able to feel, and notice what you are feeling in your body, your facial expression and your body posture. You then practise feeling this emotion. So the next time you want to choose to feel this emotion you know what facial expression to have and what your posture should be like to help you feel your desired emotion.

Furthermore remember that emotions are located in the body and by noticing what part of the body a particular emotion is usually located, you can consciously place your attention in that part of your body to help you feel another emotion. For example if the emotion of happiness is located in your heart and general centre of your body, you can place your awareness there to help you create the emotion of happiness.

Important Note:

Choosing another emotion is a useful technique whilst you are developing awareness and acceptance. The ability to choose another emotion comes out of being aware and is a step towards Pure Awareness, however, it is <u>not</u> Pure Awareness. In Pure Awareness your emotions will naturally be in alignment with beneficial actions that come from your true self and you will be at ease in the present moment.

Important Note:

At first it is probably going to be easier to be aware when you are calmly going about your normal everyday life. It is good to practise this process then. So that when you are triggered you can more easily bring awareness to the situation.

Table 4e: Choosing another emotion to lead to a more beneficial action.

Date and time	Situation	Emotion(s) that lead to next Emotion(s)	What emotion(s) did you choose?	Action.
Example	I'm dissatisfied in my job.	Dissatisfaction		
		Sercurity (from pay) ard stuckness		
		Fear and apathetic	Curiosity	Notice what you like doing at and what gives you joy and satisfaction in work and outside of work.

Step 6e

Reflect on your emotion(s) and actions to see whether you could have chosen another emotion that would have been more helpful, that is leads to an action that is more in alignment with who you are, your true self. Reflect on what you have written on **Tables 1e to 4e**.

It is helpful to step back and reflect on what your motivation for being in the situation was and what your motivation for choosing the emotion in step 5e was. You may believe that you had to choose the emotion so fast that you did not have time to consider what your motivation was. However as I have stated in the **'Important Note: Motivation'** all of your actions are a result of what is motivating you. To become aware of what was motivating you notice what emotions you had before, during and after the action.

Try to avoid justifying and analysing your emotions and actions and what is motivating them. Also try to avoid believing that the emotion was just what arose and that you had no control in it.

Important Note:

I am not saying that you have control over your emotions; I am saying that your emotions arise as a result of what is motivating your actions.

Try to settle inside of yourself and ask yourself "What was I trying to achieve? What in me was guiding my emotions and actions?" Allow the answer to arise from within you. Take your time and be honest with yourself. Acceptance of all that is arising within you is needed here. If the answer you receive is a felt sense ask yourself what this means to you? To help you do this look at part 2 of the manual, especially the part on Grounding. When you are grounded a space is created inside of you that enables you to be present and connected to your inner guidance and knowing.

Using the example above in **step 5e** you may realise that you need a feeling to help you get out of feeling apathetic and into more useful action.

enthusiastic

In the gap you choose other emotions = enthusiasm and motivation; you may still also feel fear and that is ok. Which leads to action = look at what options you have and would like to have. Remember that you are not trying to deny your emotions and at this moment you are working with the awareness that you have.

Your awareness will grow and you will work differently with your emotions as your awareness develops.

Important Note:

Over the next couple of days practice going inside of yourself and asking yourself "What was I trying to achieve? What in me was guiding my emotions and actions?" Allow the answer to arise from within you. Take your time and be honest with yourself.

Please read the **"Being Triggered"** and **"Acceptance"** sections below. After reading theses sections please continue to step 7 and follow each step to the end of the process. Steps 7 through to 9 are the same for 'thinking people' and 'feeling people' as they bring awareness of emotions and thoughts together.

Being Triggered

It will be harder to be aware when you have been triggered: Being triggered is when you start to act, feel and think as if the original experience, that could of happened a long time ago and caused a major reaction in you at the time of that experience, is happening again in this moment. The original experience was also probably traumatising. You can get "triggered" by an event, a situation, a person, a phase, an action – almost anything can trigger an unhelpful habitual response. The tale-tell signs that you have been triggered are that you do not remember what caused the strong reaction in you in the first place and / or you are experiencing an intensity of emotion and / or thoughts that do not match the reality of the situation you are in, in another words you have overreacted. See examples in **step 4** and **4e** and in **table 3** or **table 3e**, depending on which tables you are working with.

Acceptance

The process is set out like this because I want you to become aware of your thoughts, or emotions, and the effect that they have on your actions. Have you noticed that some of your thoughts, or emotions, lead to actions that are not beneficial to you and therefore cause chaos and suffering in your life?

It can take time to develop complete acceptance. Complete acceptance is only reached by knowing all that is going on inside you and this is covered in detail in part 2. Therefore it is quicker at first to notice what you are thinking, or notice your emotions, and to choose another thought, or emotion, if your previous one is not beneficial

In part 2 you learn how to become aware of your whole body, mind and emotions. You learn that when you accept what is happening inside of you, it naturally changes. Complete acceptance of what is happening inside of you, enables everything to transform and brings you into contact with who you really are in that moment; which is incredibly empowering.

However, I thought that I would mention acceptance now and I would also like you to refer to part 2 of the process after you have read this. What I mean by acceptance is allowing your thoughts and emotions to be how they are without adding extra to them by fighting, judging, blaming, analysing, making a story etc. Most people are used to adding extra as they like to feel justified, for instance, in having the thoughts and emotions that they are experiencing. By adding extra to your thoughts and feelings you are prolonging the time that you experience them and are more likely to take action that further reinforces the thought and emotion. If the thoughts and feelings are not beneficial to you, the results of your actions are likely to be not beneficial to you.

For example the other morning I noticed that the door on my car looked like it had been deliberately scratched with a sharp object. I was really angry and thoughts of who it could be rushed through my mind. I told myself "I am justified in my anger as most people would feel angry in this situation", which fuelled the anger more. As I started the car I could feel my anger rising. My first thoughts where "get rid of the anger, I cannot drive to work like this". I know different techniques of clearing emotion and could have easily used one in this moment. Instead I decided to accept the thoughts as I know that if I did not accept my thoughts they would have continued and fuelled the anger.

Acceptance freed up my energy and attention so I could completely feel my anger, without adding extra to it.

The anger intensified still. However with awareness rather than trying to do anything with the anger, it started to dissolve and I felt that I could start driving. **The anger quickly passed and I returned to balance.**

Important Note:

This example demonstrates that acceptance is a powerful way to stop the thought or emotion from increasing in strength and its grip over you. Furthermore, complete acceptance of the emotion or thought dissolves and releases the emotion or thought in you entirely and you return to balance. At first complete acceptance can take time to reach. However with practice and understanding of what acceptance is, acceptance is a quick process.

Noticing thought(s) and emotion(s) together.

Step 7

With your growing awareness and the reflecting that you have been doing, you might have become aware that with each thought that you have, there is an accompanying emotion. Or if you are more of a 'feeling' person you might have noticed that with each emotion there is an accompanying thought. Practice being aware of when you have a thought, that there is an emotion accompanying it. Alternatively when you have an emotion, that there is a thought that accompanies it. It may help to write them down with the resulting action on table 5or table 5e depending on whether you choose to change your thought(s) or emotion(s).

The benefits of noticing what thoughts and emotions may accompany each other are:

- You can stop the cycling of the thoughts and emotions much more quickly.

- You can return to balance and clarity more quickly.

- You are less likely to be triggered by the same thought(s) or emotion(s) again see **step 8**.

- Clear the energy of the thoughts and emotions that support a limited pattern of behaviour more thoroughly see **step 9**.

As emotions create chemicals in your body, you can become aware of these chemicals and by using the tools that you have gained from this process you can prevent the chemicals from growing stronger and creating reactions in your body and therefore behaviour that is not in alignment with who you really are:

For example, you can notice that you are starting to feel a certain emotion (let's say anger) before you unconsciously react from that emotion (in an angry manner). Or if you are more aware of your thoughts you can notice what thoughts are likely to lead to a certain emotion (thought = "He always does this to me" accompanying emotion = anger) and change your thoughts to "It is not personal" before you unconsciously react from that emotion (in an angry manner).

Table 5: Thoughts and accompanying Emotions

Date and Time	Situation	Thought(s)	Accompanying Emotion(s)	Action
Example	I made a mistake whilst giving a presentation.	'I am useless'	Nervousness	Clumsiness - start to knock things over / bump into things

Table 5e: Emotions and accompanying Thoughts

Date and Time	Situation	Emotion(s)	Accompanying Thought(s)	Action
Example	I made a mistake whilst giving a presentation	Nervousness	'I am useless'	Clumsiness - start to knock things over / bump into things.

Step 8

Now that you are aware that thoughts and emotions accompany each other, you can choose whether to change your thought or emotion. Choose whether it is easier to change your thought or your emotion. Write down what you chose to do with the resulting action on Table 6 or 6e, depending on whether you choose to change your thought(s) or emotion(s). Be aware of what happens. If what happens is not in alignment with who you are, you can choose again in the same situation.

Furthermore reflect on when you have done this to see if what you are choosing is in alignment with who you really are. The result of this is that:

- You will be less likely to be triggered by the same thought(s) or emotion(s) again.

With practise this process becomes very fast and effortless, that is, automatic.

The following is an example to demonstrate the power of the connection between thought(s), emotion(s), actions and behaviour:

Your thought is 'I am useless' and the accompanying emotion may be nervousness and the resulting behaviour is clumsiness; this is very likely to reinforce the thought and accompanying emotion. What tends to happen is that the next time you experience the same thought, emotion or action they will all be triggered. The more times this happens the more solid the connection of the thought, emotion and action becomes in the brain and the body. The result of this is likely to be that the next time you experience being nervous, even in a situation when it is very appropriate to be nervous, the thought that 'I am useless' may be triggered in your head and your behaviour will then be clumsy.

Important Note:

The purpose of this process is to get you consciously aware of your previous thought and emotional patterns, as conscious awareness and acceptance is needed before you can choose to change your thought and emotional patterns and conditioning. I have experienced many times, within myself and with clients, that once they are aware of their conditioning and the suffering and the chaos it creates in their lives they are happy and willing to let their thought and emotional patterns go.

You can achieve a lot by working consciously. However, if you clear and release the energy inside of you that is holding the thought and emotion patterns of your conditioning in you, they are no longer going to be a part of you or your experience.

- The benefits of this are twofold: the limiting thought or emotion will have less power over you and you will be less likely to be triggered by the same thought(s) or emotion(s) again.

In other words the connection in the brain and body will be less solid and fairly quickly you will not have the limiting belief or experience the emotion in the same limiting way as you did before.

Clearing energy inside of your body enables you to be more centered and present, in which you will experience more intuitive knowing. This is covered in detail in part 2 of Key to Awareness.

Table 6: Making a choice that will lead to a beneficial Action.

Date and Time	Situation	Thought(s)	Accompanying Emotion(s)	Action	Choice	Action
Example	I made a mistake whilst giving a presentation	'I am useless'	Nervousness	Clumsiness - start to knock things over / bump into things.	Changed Emotion to Confidence	I took a deep breath - No more clumsiness

Table 6e: Making a choice that will lead to a beneficial Action.

Situation	Emotion(s)	Accompanying Thoughts(s)	Action	Choice	Resulting Action
I made a mistake whilst giving a presentation	Nervousness	'I am useless'	Clumsiness - start to knock things over / bump into things.	Changed Thought to 'I can do this'	Payed more attention - No more clumsiness

Step 9

Have you had the experience where you have just known what to do? Rather than reacting from emotions or procrastinating over all your conscious options?

Going through this process you have probably noticed that when you have created a gap in your stream of thoughts and emotions, by being aware, the habitual need to react falls away.

At first you were probably very aware of how you would of habitually wanted to react; that is you might of felt a drive to say or behave in a certain way, that comes from your conditioning. However now you are confident that if you stay in the gap in awareness, this previously driven response fades away. In its place comes a response, that may or <u>may not</u> be verbal, that is in alignment with who you really are. **This response will arise in you, you will sense that it is true for you and you will be at ease.** The opposite of this is your mind racing around for the right response that will gain you what you want.

Record on table 7, below, when a response has arisen from inside of you and you have known what to do.

Important Note:

As you now realise that thought and emotional accompany each other you may benefit from reading the **'Thinking' people's** *or* **'Feeling' people's** **Key to Awareness process** *in the previous page that you have not read. I have purposely used the same examples so that you can see that you can* *choose to change the thought or the emotion and get the same, or a similar, action.*

Table 7: Record times when you have intuitively known what to do

Date and time	Situation	What did your awareness bring to your attention?	What happened? / What action did you take?

Part 2 Contents

Benefits of Grounding	87
How to Ground yourself	89
Why practice relaxation	93
A very simple relaxation exercise	97
Jacobson's Relaxation Method	99
Inner Resourcing	103
Intro to Releasing energy in your body exercise	105
Releasing energy in your body exercise	107
Would I benefit from seeing a therapist?	115
Bullet points for Releasing energy in body exercise	117
Checking in with yourself in busy / crowed places	121
Meditation	123
Golden Guidelines for Meditation	125

Awareness of Breath Meditation	**127**
Introduction to Pure Awareness Exercise	**129**
Pure Awareness	**133**
Alternative Method – Clearing and Cleaning	**137**
Appendixes	**141**
An example of how someone became aware of how they were stuck:	**141**
Free Resources	**145**

Part 2 of the "Key to Awareness" process.

Part 2 is about processing the energy in your body that is caused by your thought(s), emotion(s), thought patterns, emotional patterns, actions and conditioning and thus releasing it. This enables you to be more present in your body and therefore more present in the moment and have a deeper sense of awareness.

You will learn how to connect with the whole of your body. There is no greater connection than that which you have with your body. As this opens up your ability to have a deeper connection with yourself, others and the world; through you becoming to know what it is like to listen to your intuition and then trusting to act from your intuition. This gives your experiences depth and makes them more fulfilling and meaning for you.

This part of the process is also presented in a logical order. In each exercise you focus on grounding, then your body sensations and then your breath to bring you into awareness. In the "realising energy in your body" exercise you first focus on your body sensations to help you open up to whatever arises within your awareness. By practising all of the exercises you will experience that awareness, and therefore acceptance, your body sensations, mind / perceptions and energy naturally shifts and changes. This shift enables everything to transform and brings you into contact with who you really are; which is incredibly empowering.

When you have read through each technique and practised it at least seven times, you will naturally find it more beneficial to use some techniques rather than others. I want you to make each of these techniques your own. What I mean by this is that after following the instructions several times I want you to go with your growing sense of awareness and do what you sense is right for you in the moment that you are doing the exercise.

The final exercise of "Pure Awareness" is less directive. You are encouraged to allow whatever arises in your body, mind and heart to simply be there; there is no need to 'do' anything. You will notice in awareness that thoughts, emotions and sensations arises and fall. You have no goal; you are simply resting in pure awareness. In this space of pure awareness you will come to rest in your true essence.

As you develop through this process and continue to develop your awareness you will notice that more and more you are resting in your true and real self during your everyday life and in all that you do.

<u>**Important Note:**</u>

The purpose of each exercise is to completely release any energy that was previously stuck in your body. When energy is completely released you do not experience that energy and any previous trigger you may have experienced from that energy again. Do what you sense is right for you to release energy, without losing the purpose of the exercise.

Grounding

The benefits of Grounding:

- It is the quickest way to become aware.
- Gain clarity.
- Feel connected to the whole of yourself: body, mind and heart.
- Feel connected to the ground, the earth and nature.
- Have clear access to your intuition.
- Feel stronger and more alive.
- Helps you gain a wider perspective and acceptance.
- Have more energy and vitality.

Everyone that I have taught grounding to has said that they have felt a tremendous benefit from being able to ground themselves.

I believe that grounding lays the foundations for everything else. That is why I have chosen it as the first exercise in part 2 of the manual. However, I recognise that some people may find this difficult and would benefit from some relaxation exercises first.

Being able to ground yourself is essential to being aware. I do not believe that you can be aware without being grounded.

What Grounding is not:

- Not leaving your body
- Not floating
- Not daydreaming
- Not closing down
- Not 'playing' memories in your head
- Not acting out old habits

Grounding is:

- Being aware of your body and feeling connected to your body
- Being aware of the energy in your body
- Feeling the wholeness and togetherness of your body
- Feeling the earth
- Feeling part of the earth
- Opening up

Practice the following grounding technique at least twice per day and whenever you feel like you need to. It may take 5 minutes to do this exercise at first, please be patient and practise all the steps in this exercise. You will become very quick at grounding. With practice you will be able to ground yourself instantly. This is one exercise that I would not like you to change until you have felt the full benefits of being grounded. **Practice this daily.**

How to ground yourself

- Take some time to sit comfortably with both feet in contact with the floor.

- Become aware of your breath.

- Allow yourself to notice your breath, without trying to control it.

- Relax and enjoy the sensation of your breath entering and leaving your body.

- After a while bring your awareness to your feet, they may become warm and / or tingle, if it helps also stay aware of your breath.

- Give yourself time to become fully aware of your feet.
- It might help to ask yourself "How do my feet feel on the ground?"

- If you are wearing shoes "How do my feet feel in my shoes?" By bringing your attention to your feet, more blood will go to your feet and you may feel them becoming warm.

- When you can feel your feet and your attention is in your feet, gently allow your attention to remain in your feet and at the same time slowly come up your lower legs,

- Wait until your attention is in your feet and lower legs. Then slowly proceed to extend your attention to your knees, your thighs, your pelvis,

- Become aware that your attention is now in your lower legs, knees, thighs and pelvis.

- your lower torso, your mid torso, your upper torso,

- your shoulders, your arms, your hands,

- your neck, your throat, your head, - the sides, top and middle,

- and finally your face, eyes, ears, nose and mouth.

- Until you are aware of the whole of your body.

- You may feel your body becoming warm and / or tingling.

- Keeping the awareness of the whole of your body, imagine about 5 to 10% of your energy (it may help you to visualise the roots of a tree, or pieces of string) extending from your feet and your pelvis into the ground.

- It is <u>important</u> that your energy and <u>awareness remains in your body as well as extending into the ground</u>.

- Give yourself time do this slowly and allow it to happen.

- If any thoughts or emotions arise gently bring your attention back to the energy in your body; gently letting go of everything else.

- Then with your awareness of the energy in the whole of your body allow about 5 to 10% of your energy to extend into the ground, from your feet and pelvis.

- Doing this connects you with earth and cleans your energy.

- After a while you will probably feel energy coming up from the ground into your body, and you may feel your body tingling, becoming warm and / or a sense of expansion.

- Allow the energy from the ground to extend to the whole of your body. The energy from the ground becomes your energy as it enters your body.

- The energy from the ground brings aliveness and vitality into you.

- Stay with being connected with the ground for as long as you can.

Why practice relaxation

In today's world people are forced into believing that they have to be doing something every moment of the day. Work hours are getting longer and the work demands are increasing. Now more than ever it is important to take time out to relax.

- Relaxation is one of the most valuable skills you can require.

- It is the body's natural way to slow down.

- Relaxation is a physical skill that needs to be practiced.

- It has an immediate effect and long term benefits.

- Relaxation calms the mind and gives you a different perspective on life and enables you to live in a more effective way; which leads to Awareness.

Guidelines for relaxation

❖ As relaxation slows down your body and clears your mind you will be more effective at any given task after you have taken some time out to relax.

- ❖ After relaxing you will be an easier person to be around, so relax for the other people in your life, if it feels too selfish to do it for yourself.

- ❖ Try to set aside a specific time of day for your regular practice, if possible. Some people find it easier to have their day structured.

- ❖ At first it would be helpful to practice twice a day. Even if you can only spare one minute, you will quickly notice the benefits.

- ❖ If you can, choose a quiet place. It is easier to learn to relax if you are not interrupted by loud sounds, the telephone or people. Soon you will be able to relax and slow your body down even in noisy, busy environments.

- ❖ Just enjoy doing the relaxation, do not worry if you are doing everything right, there is no "right" or "wrong". All that matters is Awareness of what is.

- ❖ Choose a place with a comfortable temperature and cover yourself with a blanket if needed. It is harder to relax if you are too hot or too cold.

- ❖ Use cushions to support your body's natural curvature of the spine: in a chair place cushions at your lower back and neck if needed.

- ❖ For lying place a good sized cushion under your knees to ease any tension in your lower back; this often eliminates the need for a cushion under your head, which ensures a more natural position for the spine.

- ❖ Try to have your body in a straight line.

- ❖ Sit and relax if you have just had a meal, rather than lying down.

- ❖ Avoid practising when you are hungry.

- ❖ It may be helpful to set yourself a time limit to relax and set a watch or timer, with a gentle tone, to let you know when the time has passed.

Afterwards

- ❖ As your body has slowed down, avoid jumping up as this will result in you feeling dizzy.

- ❖ Always use the quick relaxation method at the end - Stretch –Yawn – Wiggle – and have a lazy look around you.

- ❖ Say to yourself, "I will keep this feeling of calm / peace / tranquillity with me throughout my day".

- ❖ Remove any support cushions from under your body that you may be using, before you get up.

- ❖ If lying down, roll onto your side and use your arms to push yourself into a sitting position. Then, if on the floor, get slowly onto one knee and then stand up.

- ❖ Then move and speak and breathe a little more gently then usual for a while afterwards. Then proceed with your day.

- ❖ As your muscles have been softened by the relaxation it is important to be gentle with yourself for a while after the relaxation and be careful when first using your muscles again.

Below is a very simple and short series of movements that helps aid relaxation.

Stretch   Stretch the body and all its limbs gently in all directions.

Yawn   To stretch the facial muscles and initiate the feeling of relaxation.

Wriggle   Wriggle gently all parts of the body.

Relax   Relax the entire body and limbs.

Important Note:

One of the easiest ways to relax is to become aware of your breath. Do not try to control your breath; just bring your awareness to it. Your breath is extra special as it is the only system in the body that can work involuntary, i.e. without your conscious

Jacobson's Relaxation Method.

The purpose of the Jacobson's modified relaxation is to increase awareness of muscular tension. It does this by getting you to tense your muscles slightly and then letting go of the tension. The overall aim is to relate the tension you feel in your body to everyday situations so that you can release your tension at will.

- Make yourself comfortable. Breathe in, hold the breath, recognising the overall tension. Breath out, recognising the overall relaxation.

- Gently bring the toes up towards the knees- hold -and let go.

- Gently press the heels into the floor- hold -and let go.

- Bring your knees together- hold -and let go.

- Tighten the buttocks- hold -and let go.

- Gently pull your stomach towards your spine- hold -and let go.

- Bring your shoulders up towards your ears- only enough to feel the tension- hold -and let go.

- Bring your elbows and upper arms into your sides- hold -and let go.

- Make a fist with your hands - gently clench- hold -and let go.

- Point your chin forward- hold -and let go.

- Clench your teeth together - hold -and let your jaw drop down slightly.

- Press your lips together and then release the tension so they are hardly touching.

- Press your tongue on the top of your mouth-- hold -and let go.

- Close your eyes tightly- hold -and let go.

- Frown a little- hold -and let go. Look surprised- hold -and let go.

- Now enjoy the feeling of less tension, trying to let go more with each breath.

- ALLOW YOURSELF TIME TO RELAX.

- Gently move your fingers then toes. Wiggle a little, yawn, then stretch and when you are ready, open your eyes.

Slowly proceed with what you are doing,

trying to stay more relaxed.

Inner Resourcing

I learnt about internal and external resourcing from Franklin Sills when I studied Biodynamic Craniosacral Therapy. An external resource is something you do to change your mood to usually feel good, however it can also be used to create another mood. For example, you may find that listening to particular music, talking to friends, exercising or going for a walk in nature helps you to feel good.

Internal resource is a sense inside of yourself that feels "good", resourceful, to you. The purpose of this exercise is to bring your mind and body into the present moment and feel resourced within yourself.

Below are the steps I use to obtain an inner resource within myself and with my clients. I find that it often helps to bring people through the grounding process first.

- Sit or lie down so that you are comfortable. If you usually find yourself going to sleep when you are lying down it may be helpful to sit up.

- Bring your attention to your breath.

- Slowly bring your attention into your body (if you find this difficult please see a therapist).

- Ask yourself "Where in my body feels comfortable right now?" Allow the answer to come to you; it may take a little time.

- It does not matter if this area is really small, like the tip of your finger, or large like your back.

- Bring your attention to this area of your body and ask yourself "What is it about this area that feels resourceful?" Again, allow the answer to come to you, it may take a little time.

- Without judgement or analysing, accept whatever is resourceful to you and take notice of how that feels and your general sense of it. It may be a feeling of relaxation, joy, easiness or it may be more of a sense of peace, freedom, acceptance etc.

- Whatever it is allow your attention to rest there.

- Allow the feeling and or sense to just be.

- What usually happens that the sense and / or feeling in this area will spread throughout your body.

- Enjoy a sense of resourcefulness in your body for as long as you have time to.

See if you can keep a part of your attention on this feeling and / or sense for the rest of the day.

Introduction to Releasing energy in your body exercise.

Use this exercise to release energy in your body and gain insight into how you respond to situations in life. Use this exercise daily and also whenever you are feeing stuck. I use this exercise myself, I teach it to my clients and I run workshops on how to use this exercise. I developed this exercise from learning meditation, "Focusing" and Biodynamic Craniosacral Therapy.

Use this exercise to:

- Pay attention to your inner body
- Get in touch with your feelings
- Listen to your body's sense of how you are
- Gain insight into how you respond to situations in life
- Release stuck energy from your body and mind
- Increase your awareness
- Increase your vitality

Find a quite place where you will not be disturbed and leave your mobile phone turned off, in another place.

It will benefit you immensely if you read through the releasing energy exercise before you start doing the exercise. Do this for at least the first three times you do the exercise.

As you become familiar with the exercise, the shifts and releases in your body and mind can happen very quickly.

You will then be able to check in with yourself regularly and in busy and crowded places without much trouble; see guidelines at the end of the exercise for how to do this.

At first your body's sense may be unclear and vague; however, if you continue to pay attention to it the energy will open up, often revealing insights about how you are. Your insights may be in words, a sense, feelings and / or pictures. Whatever you get is right for you in that moment.

You will then experience a shift in your body that frees up your energy and results in you experiencing situations differently: that is from a freer more open space internally in your body and externally in your behaviour and how others respond to you.

What follows are the eight steps of this process.

Important Note:

These seven steps are for your guidance only and are to be used as guidelines only, in that they are not to be strictly followed. You are encouraged to follow your own intuition and go with what you intuitively sense you need to do.

Releasing energy in your body exercise.

Ground

You may do this sitting or lying down. If you are familiar with grounding ground yourself. Alternatively follow the **grounding** exercise to ground yourself.

Inner resourcing

Do the inner resourcing exercise. Stay with the feeling or sense for as long as you need to, to be able to go back to the feeling if you are finding this process difficult.

Go Inside and settle.

Gently allow your attention to deepen further into your body, allowing yourself to feel everything in the whole of your body. You might not really feel anything or you might feel lots of things. Just allow yourself to settle into feeling your whole body. If you notice that there is an area of your body that you cannot feel, this is ok and is a part of the exercise for you in this moment. Let any thoughts go, without getting involved in them. The aim of this exercise is to be in your body and noticing what sensations and feelings you have, rather than being in your mind with your thoughts. If this is difficult go to the area of your body where your inner resource is. Then when you are ready allow your attention to deepen further into your body.

Notice what you feel and if any concerns arise. Just acknowledge each concern that arises and let it pass. Do not get involved in it, just let it pass. It may help to imagine putting each concern to one side, out of the way. Some people find it helps to make a list of their concerns using their imagination. For example they might imagine "their concerns" being written on a list in front of them, and then put this list to one side. The aim is to settle into your body and clear some inner space, before you go to the next step.

Ask yourself "What do I feel most, what wants my attention?"

You will notice that the feelings in one part of your body come to the foreground and your attention goes to that area. <u>DO NOT GET LOST IN IT</u>: Do not become the feeling; this means do not get into the emotion, whether it be anger or joy. Instead notice what is there with a light-hearted attention and curiosity. This also means that you do not allow your mind to take over and tell you a story about the feeling. There will probably be lots of things to think about – too many, let them go. Allow yourself to feel all that is there. Allow yourself to feel all the unclear feelings that are there. Staying grounded and present is the best way to do this; If needed go back to the area of your body where your inner resource is. Than expand your attention out to the whole of your body. When you are ready ask yourself "What do I feel most, what wants my attention?"

At first, this place in your body is likely to be in the place that you generally feel things.

What is the body's sense?

Ask yourself what is the quality of all that you are feeling. Let a word, sense, phrase or image arise from the feeling. For example, the word may be tightness, stuck, sadness, grief, blocked, restricted, rigid or a phase or an image. Stay with the feeling until the word, sense, image or phase fits what you are feeling just right. What I mean by stay with the feeling is having a mental sense of curiosity rather than trying to become the feeling (for example becoming angry) or do something with the feeling, like grasp hold of it, change it or judge yourself for it.

If after some time a word, image or phase does not arise try the alternative method below:

Ask yourself "If the feeling had a shape, colour or symbol what it would be?" Allow this to come to you, do not think about it. A shape, colour or symbol will naturally arise. I have never done this process with someone that did not have a shape or colour for what they were feeling.

I have found that by using a word or phrase people often slip into the content of what they believe the feeling is about. Alternatively they can go into fantasy. However, some people need more content to provide them with more insight about themselves. I believe that with trust in the process, which comes from practice, you can gain insight and release thoughts, emotions, conditioning, trauma and behaviour patterns without the need for content. Therefore, I prefer to do this process free from all content, which includes labeling the feelings.

Important Note:

Allow everything to arise without judgment or criticism. Trust that what you need to gain insight from and release will happen without you trying to control the process.

If what arises is too frightening to be with, stay on the edge of the feeling. As if the place in your body where the feeling is were a pond and you are standing at the edge of the pond looking at it. Give yourself a little time to see if you can explore the feeling from this 'distance'. Do this with a light-hearted curiosity. When you have settled, go through **'What is the body's sense?'** part of this exercise.

If it is still too frightening or traumatising please speak to a therapist; see **"Would I benefit from seeing a therapist?"** at the end of this exercise.

Resonate

You will know when it fits just right because the feeling will intensify or relax a little, this is like an "ah ha" experience. You will only know this if you can stay with the feeling and let the words, phase or image arise at the same time, rather than getting lost in the mental process of thinking about it. Stay with the feeling.

If you are working with a colour or a shape just simply notice that until it shifts.

Clarity

Stay with the feeling and the word, phase or image (colour or shape) until you sense a shift in the feeling. This shift may be sensed as a greater or less intensity of the feeling or the feeling may move to another body part, or you may experience something different. What is required is that you allow the body to do what it needs to do.

To help the shift you may need to ask yourself "Why do I feel (body's sense or colour or shape). What is important here?" Again allow the answer to come from the feeling. If you get an answer and you do not sense a shift in the feeling, then allow that kind of answer to go and gently return to the felt sense in your body. Then gently ask yourself again.

Let whatever wants to arise from the body's sense arise and "speak" to you. When this happens the body's sense will shift. This shift tells you that you have internally processed something. You may feel expansion or relief or something else.

Sometimes the shift will be so small that it is hardly noticeable, especially when you first start practising this releasing energy exercise. However, if you take your time and pay attention to your body and listen to what it has to tell you a shift will take place.

You know the body's sense has shifted when the original word, phase or image (colour or shape) does not fit it anymore.

Receiving

Let yourself receive and acknowledge the process as it is.

Important Note:

Insight is not always conscious; that is you might not always be consciously aware of the changes you are making. Trust that as the energy in your body is released so is the conditioning, along with the thought and emotional patterns and actions that went with it. The result of this is that your thought and emotional patterns and actions naturally change and this may not become conscious until you or someone else notices that you have changed.

Give yourself time and ask your body if there is anything else that you need to know or if it is ok to end the session now. Give this a little time. If you need to stay then do. With acceptance things can shift and change very quickly.

It may be ok to end the session now; however, you may sense that you have not received all you need to know and that a bigger shift can take place. If you are able to, stay with the exercise. If you need to end the exercise now, thank your body and promise yourself that you will give this felt sense some more time soon.

Important Note:

Read through the whole exercise before you do it, for the first three times at least. Overleaf is a bullet point list of the exercise to use whilst you are doing the exercise to act as a reminder of what you need to do. After you have done the exercise a few times it may help you to do your own bullet point list to use as a reminder. Remember that theses steps and bullet points are only guidelines and that you are encouraged to follow your own intuition and go with what you intuitively sense you need to do.

<u>Would I benefit from seeing a therapist?</u>

The answer is yes if you are:

- Having trouble feeling your body
- Cannot feel parts of your body after you have done all the exercises in part 2 of Key to Awareness and this exercise three times
- You are finding this exercise frightening
- Trauma has surfaced doing this exercise

I would recommend seeing a Biodynamic Craniosacral Therapist, an Energetic NLP practitioner or a therapist that is recommended from talking to a friend or other professional about what you are experiencing.

Releasing energy in your body exercise, bullet notes:

Find a quite place where you will not be disturbed.

Ground

- Familiarise yourself with the grounding exercise.

Inner resourcing

- Do the inner resourcing exercise.
- Stay with the feeling or sense for as long as you need to, to be able to go back to the feeling if you are finding this process difficult.

Go Inside and settle.

- Allow yourself to settle into feeling your whole body.
- Let any thoughts go, without getting involved in them.
- Be in your body and noticing what sensations and feelings you have.
- Keep settling deeper into your body.

Ask yourself "What do I feel most, what wants my attention?"

- Stay with the part of your body that comes to the foreground.
- Notice what is there with a light-hearted attention and curiosity.

- When you are ready ask yourself "What do I feel most, what wants my attention?"

What is the body's sense?

- Ask yourself what is the quality of all that you are feeling.
- Let a word, sense, phrase or image arise from the feeling.
- Alternatively ask yourself "If the feeling had a shape, colour or symbol what it would be?"
- Stay with the feeling until the word, sense, image or phase fits what you are feeling just right.

Resonate

- You will know when it fits just right because the feeling will intensify or relax a little, this is like an "ah ha" experience.
- If you are working with a colour or a shape just simply notice that until it shifts.

Clarity

- Let whatever wants to arise from the body's sense arise and "speak" to you.
- You know the body's sense has shifted when the original word, phase or image (colour or shape) does not fit it anymore.

Receiving

- Let yourself receive and acknowledge the process as it is.
- Give yourself time and ask your body if there is anything else that you need to know or if it is ok to end the session now.

With acceptance things can shift and change very quickly.

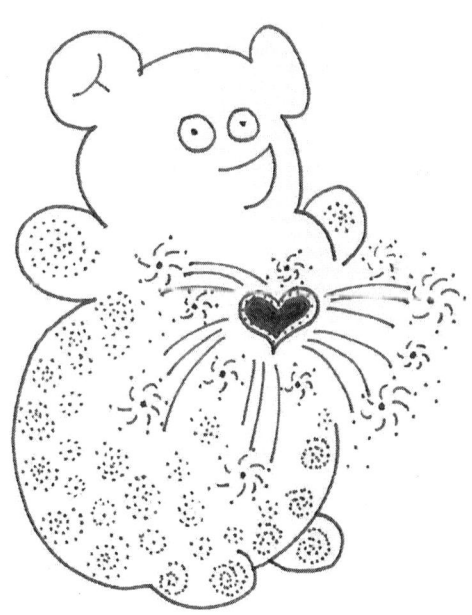

Checking in with yourself in busy and crowed places:

You can only do this when you are familiar and happy with the exercise.

When you have done this exercise at least six times in a safe, comfortable and quiet place you might feel able to try it in other places. When previously doing the exercise you might have noticed that your body has felt like it has expanded outside of you as well as internally. This is probably because you have expanded your awareness into your energy field and allowed your body to relax more into your energy field. I love this feeling of relaxation and expansion. My clients often tell me that is feels very freeing at the time and the sense of freedom lasts throughout the day if not longer.

It is important to be aware of your energy field when you are out and about and more so when you are doing this exercise in public places. Your energy field is the space around your body. Some people think your energy field is the same as your aura or your personal space; this is a good way to think of it but it is not the same thing. Some people unconsciously have a very large energy field; have you ever met someone who seems larger than life? This is probably because their energy field extends out to a large space around them.

To get more of a sense of energy fields ask a friend if you can sense their energy field. Do this my standing about three feet away from your friend and move your hand slowly towards, then away, from their body. Try doing this further away and closer to your friend, to see if your sense of their energy field changes. At the same time ask your friend to close their eyes and notice, but not tell you, when they can sense you. When they sense you, you will be in their energy field. See if what you feel matches when they sense you. Remember to have fun with this and it will be easier to sense energy fields.

Alternatively, in your own home imagine having your energy field extending all around you like a sphere at different distances, for example 8, 6, 4 and 2 feet. What distance feels more comfortable to you?

In public spaces I would advise that you have your energy field at a distance of 3ft all around you. In busy and crowd spaces reduce your energy field to 2ft all around you, especially when you are doing this exercise. The reason for this is that you especially do not want other people's energy entering your energy field and body when you are doing this exercise.

Imagine that your energy field has a <u>semi-permeable</u> membrane, i.e. a layer that allows some things through but not others, that is set to allow energy and information that is "good" for you i.e. healthy, vitality giving, joyful emotions, information about your children, and reflects away from you energy and information that is "less good" for you.

Meditation

The purpose of meditation is to be and to bring this awareness of being into all of your activities.

Meditation is about being:

Being where you are,

Being in the moment,

Accepting what is there inside of you.

Meditating is a great way of gaining awareness about your body, mind, and behaviour. That is why I would like to mention it here. However, I am not stating that you have to meditate to be aware. If you have followed each step in part 1 of this manual and practiced the exercises in part 2, I am sure that you have gained a great deal of awareness.

Important Note:

In essence any exercise that enables you to get in touch with what is inside you and expand your awareness of yourself is meditation.

There are lots of different ways to meditate that focus on different aspects of yourself and spiritual practices; there are far too many to try to cover them as part of this manual. This is purely a very brief introduction to meditation that I know you will find useful.

<u>Meditation Myths:</u>

Meditation is about having no thoughts:

This is impossible. You will experience gaps of silence in your thoughts and they will come back. It is more about the quality of your thoughts. With practice your mind will quieten and you will have less mental chatter and habitual patterns of thought. You will start to have clearer more substantial thoughts, in that you will gain insight from them.

You have to believe in Buddhism or something spiritual, or yoga to meditate:

You do not need to believe in anything to meditate. However, it is true that meditation is part of many spiritual traditions.

You have to be a certain kind of person to meditate:

Anyone can learn to and benefit from meditating. The purpose of meditation is to be who you are and gain more awareness. Trying to be a certain way or be someone else is not what meditation is about.

Golden Guidelines for meditation

- Meditate with an open, compassionate and kind state of mind and simply be with yourself.
- Take time to gain a comfortable posture that enables you to have a straight and relaxed spine; whether sitting, standing or walking.
- Try to have your back unsupported, as this helps you remain alert and will strengthen your back muscles and improve your posture.
- Decide on your object of concentration and stay with it throughout the meditation.
- Decide on your method of concentration and stay with it throughout the meditation.
- Keep in mind the purpose of meditation is to be and to bring this awareness of being into all of your activities.
- If you have a goal to achieve from the meditation, such as to relax, you are not meditating.

Important Note:

A state of being in which you are accepting where you are and what is happening inside you in your body, mind and heart, is a totally different way of experiencing yourself and life, from trying to change what you feel or wanting things to be any different, which comes from a state of 'doing'.

Being, by accepting who you are, leads to deep relaxation, even though meditation is not about relaxation (or any other goal). The result of being with yourself and not fighting what you are feeling or trying to be something other than what you are in that moment, is a deep sense of relaxation and peace.

Being, rather than doing, leads to valuable insights. These insights are more valuable if you persist with meditation and discover them yourself.

Important Note:

If the same thought or group of thoughts keep arising this can be an indication that this is important for you. Either write on a piece of paper the thought and what may need to be done or stop the meditation and deal with the task. Return to the meditation afterwards.

Awareness of Breathing Meditation

As previously mentioned your breath is a brilliant meditation object as observing your breath can relax you very quickly and it is readily available.

- Sit comfortably in a chair or on the floor:

- Try to be self supporting your back (this helps you to stay alert).
- If you can close your eyes, or you can keep them open slightly and unfocused.

- Become aware of how your body feels, where it is making contact and supported by other objects.

- Spend a minute or two focusing on these sensations.

- Become aware of your breath entering and leaving your body.

- Place one hand over your belly

- Observe what happens to your belly as you breathe in and out,

- You may notice that your belly rises with your in breath and falls with an out breath.
- Just notice, there is no need to control your breath.
- Allow the breath to come and go.

- Pay attention to how your body changes as you breathe in and out.

- It may help to focus your attention on a different part of your body, such as your nostrils.

- Rest here in the awareness of your breath.

- When the mind wanders

- Remind yourself that this is what happens when you are in the 'doing mode'.

- Simply and gently bring your attention back to breathing.

- It may help notice what the mind was doing and softly say this to yourself:

  Thinking, thinking

  Worrying, worrying

  Judging, judging

  Planning, planning

  Organising, organising etc

As soon as you notice that your mind has wondered, congratulate yourself that you have come back into awareness and notice your breath.

Introduction to Pure Awareness Exercise.

When you trust that in awareness, and therefore acceptance, your body sensations, mind / perceptions and energy naturally shift and change, and this brings you into contact with your true essence / who you really are; you are ready to practice the exercise of "Pure Awareness".

Your true essence holds the truth of who you are; it contains your full potential, that is everything you are and everything you can be. Your true essence is a direct manifestation of Life Force, Nature, God, Buddha (please insert your believes) in that it is Life Force. The answers to life are within your true essence.

Whilst doing this exercise if thought, memory and / or emotion becomes too strong and is frightening, go into your inner resource and relax. When you feel able deepen into the sense of your whole body and then connect with your whole body and therefore true essence.

If you sense that the same energy is starting to arise again you can return to your inner resource and either stay there or go to the edge of it and 'look' at the energy from there; see **What is the body's sense?** above in the "Releasing energy in your body exercise".

Important Note:

Remember that insights are not always conscious and you may only notice that something has changed when someone else points it out to you.

Pure Awareness.

Follow these steps to Pure Awareness:

1. Get comfortable sitting or lying down.
2. Get into contact with your body, you may like to do this by becoming grounded.
3. Deepen into the contact you have with your body, it may help to become aware of an inner resource.

4. Allow yourself to become aware of the whole of your body.

5. You may have the sense that that you are becoming whole.

6. That's right as you become whole you are you coming into contact with your true essence.

7. There is no need to do anything.

8. Stay in contact with your body and deepen into it, expanding your awareness of your true essence in the present moment.

9. If you find yourself drifting of into thoughts or memories stay in contact with your body in the here and now and allow them to arise and fall.

10. If emotions arise allow them to pass through the body. You may experience the emotion in its full glory or you may just sense that something has arisen within you.

11. The thought, memory and / or emotion may pass through you gently or your physical body may twitch, jerk, spasm and / or move; allow the energy that was previously stuck to move out of your body.

12. You may become aware of the space in which all your experiences, that is thoughts, perceptions and emotions, arise. This space is awareness itself. Awareness, like space, has no boundaries, edges or limits.

13. You may find that in pure awareness your senses of boundaries and limits, physical and mental, have gone.

14. Remember that shifts can be huge and very noticeable or subtle. Energy can be released from you that may seem insignificant at the time, and yet it will create major positive changes in the way you perceive and act in your life.

15. Stay in the space of Pure Awareness for as long as you can.

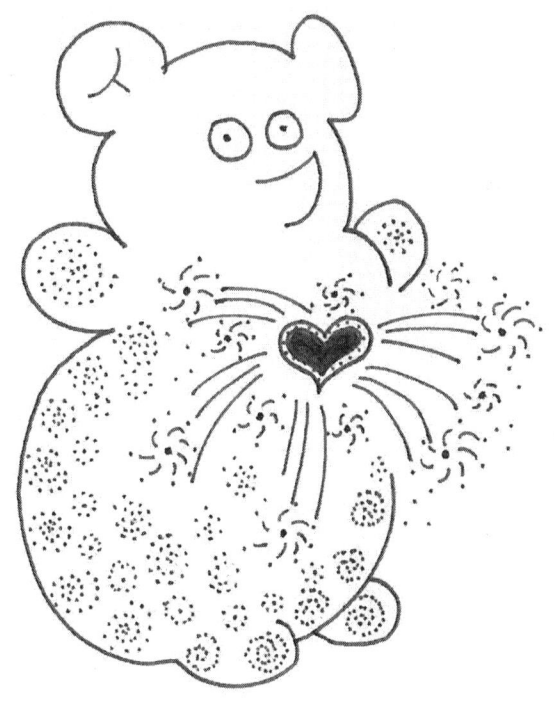

Keep practising and

You will become fully aware

and be able to

Create the Life You want to Live

Below is an alternative way to ground and clear your energy at the same time:

Grounding - Clearing and Cleaning

- Sit comfortably with your back upright and your feet on the floor.

- Imagine the earth, from out of space.

- See the core of the earth and the continents and sea surrounding the core.

- In the core of the earth is a magnet that keeps you on the surface of the earth.

- You have your feet on the surface of the earth, the ground.

- Feel; imagine the magnet beaming onto the soles of your feet, opening the energy channels on the sole of your feet.

- As the magnet opens the energy channels it is clearing and cleaning your energy.

- Take time to feel this, or imagine this happening.

- Then feel / visualise / imagine the magnet clearing and cleaning the energy in your feet.

- The energy of the magnet goes to your lower legs, clearing and cleaning your energy.

- Magnet goes to your knees, clearing and cleaning your energy.

- Into your thighs, clearing and cleaning your energy.

- Into your pelvis, clearing and cleaning your energy; allow more time for this.

- Into your lower torso, clearing and cleaning your energy.

- Into organs in your lower torso, clearing and cleaning your energy.

- Into your middle torso, clearing and cleaning your energy.

- Into your organs in your middle torso, clearing and cleaning your energy.

- Into your upper torso, clearing and cleaning your energy.

- Into organs in your upper torso, clearing and cleaning your energy; allow more time.

- Into your shoulders, clearing and cleaning your energy.

- Into your arms, clearing and cleaning your energy.

- Into your hands, clearing and cleaning your energy.

- Into your neck, clearing and cleaning your energy.

- Into your throat, clearing and cleaning your energy.

- Into the back of the bottom of your head, clearing and cleaning your energy.

- Into the back of the middle of your head, clearing and cleaning your energy.

- Into your face, clearing and cleaning your energy.

- Into the top of the back of your head, clearing and cleaning your energy.

- Into the top of your head, clearing and cleaning your energy.

- Into your forehead, clearing and cleaning your energy.

- Into your eyes, clearing and cleaning your energy.

- Into your ears, clearing and cleaning your energy.

- Into your nose, clearing and cleaning your energy.

- Into your mouth, clearing and cleaning your energy.

- Allow yourself to feel the whole of your body.

- Allow any other energy that may need to be cleared and cleaned to be.

- Stay with your new sense of wholeness, vitality and health for as long as you can.

Appendixes

<u>An example of how someone became aware of how they were stuck:</u>

One of the people that tried out this manual before it was published thought that he could not work with the steps in the manual and notice things at his work place, i.e. he thought he could not be aware at work. He said that he was noticing things when not at work and he was going through the steps. Out of curiosity I asked him what step he was on. He replied that he was on step 7.

Important Note:

The purpose of the manual is to bring awareness to all of your everyday activities – your whole life, not just part the parts of your life you feel comfortable with and find it easy to be aware of yourself and your actions.

To help him access his own awareness of what he was doing *I asked him,*

"When did you first become aware of the thought that you could not 'work through the manual' at work?"

"In step 3 and 4."

"Great you are aware of your thought patterns at work. Can you tell me more of the thought pattern?" **His reply was:**

I'm too busy at work to notice things >> I can only notice things in my spare time. >> It would be great to be in a workshop, I could do it then.

"Good. Have you had similar thought patterns before?"

"Mmm… Yes, I don't have time at work to do what I want to do."

"Has becoming 'aware' of your thought pattern changed what you think about work and / or your actions at work?"

Defensively he replied:

"I told you I am too busy at work to do anything else but work."

"Yes I know that you are very busy at work and you have told me that you are aware of your thought patterns at work so you have completed step 3 at work, well done. You have also noticed that you have had similar thought patterns before. Have you noticed how you are at work, what is your general level of motivation? What is it like being at work?"

"I just get on with what I have to do…It's like I am on automatic Pilot ….I don't want to be at work and I do not want to notice what I am thinking. I can't just quit my job"

"Yes, I understand that. Have you noticed that other things have changed when you have brought awareness to them?"

"Yes. Sometimes just being aware of it, changes it. Sometimes when I am aware I notice that I can think differently about it."

"Great, you have noticed that by choosing a different thought the situation changes. Could you notice your thoughts at work and choose a different thought?"

"I could try"

"Ok image that you are at work now and you are too busy to notice things, noticing this is bring awareness to it, what thought could you choose instead?"

"To notice my thoughts and pay attention to them to see if I can chose another more beneficial thought. Rather than just making excuses, which is something I do."

"How would that be?"

"I think that, I hope that, it would change what I think about work and my experience at work"

"Brilliant, stay with step 5 and keep choosing more beneficial thoughts for at least two whole work days. Take your time with each step to bring awareness to everything that is happening. When you are ready move onto step 6."

In summary, he was making excuses for not wanting to be aware of the fact that he is not happy in his job. He was also aware that making excuses is a pattern of his. He had the sense that he was stuck in his work place and therefore ran his old defensive behaviour programme of refusing to bring awareness into the stuck and uncomfortable part of his life.

If you take your time with each step and apply it to all areas of your life you will notice the benefits of being aware. It is easier to make changes when you are aware of what needs to be changed. To choose another thought is easy and it is amazing how much of a difference changing the way you think about something can make; see Important Note on perceptions for more information.

Free Resources

Tables

I have printed the manual A5 to make it easier for you to carry with you. I appreciate that the tables may be easier to use in a different size:

To receive copies of the tables please email me at fiona.realenergy@gmail.com

Alternatively get in touch via my website

www.RealEnergy4All.com

Free advice and exercises:

Are available on my website, let me know what else you would like.

Audio Tracks of exercises

To purchase the audio tracks that are recordings of most of the exercises in Part 2 of this process please go to:

http://realenergy4all.com/products/

Stay in touch, I look forward to hearing how you get on.

References

Gendlin, E. T. Focusing. Bantam Books. 1987

Paramananda. Change Your Mind. Windhorse Publications. 1996

Sills, F. Craniosacral Biodynamics Vol 1. North Atlantic Books. 2004

Ajahn Sumedho, Intuitive Awareness. Amaravati Buddhist Monastery. 2004

Williams, M., et al. The Mindful Way though Depression. The Guildford Press. 2004

Edward de Bono. How to have a Beautiful Mind. Vermilion. 2004